COOKING ON A STICK

Campfire Recipes for Kids

"I'm hungry!"

Linda White

Illustrated by Fran Lee

GIBBS·SMITH PUBLISHER

Salt Lake City

12 11 10 09   19 18 17 16

Published by
Gibbs Smith, Publisher
PO Box 667
Layton, UT 84041

Design by Fran Lee
Printed and bound in Korea

**Note: Some of the activities suggested in this book require adult supervision and
assistance in order to be performed safely. While many rules and safety precau-
tions have been noted throughout the book, readers are reminded to use caution
when cooking or lighting fires. The publisher is not responsible for specific
results achieved using these methods.**

Library of Congress Cataloging-in-Publication Data

White, Linda, 1948-
    Cooking on a stick: campfire recipes for kids / Linda White :
illustrated by Fran Lee. -- 1st ed.
        p. cm.
    Summary : Describes the basic procedures and equipment needed in
preparing and cooking simple foods in an outdoor setting.
    ISBN 10 : 0-87905-727-0 ISBN 13 : 978-0-87905-727-5
    1. Outdoor cookery--Juvenile literature. 2. Outdoor cookery.
I. Lee, Fran , Ill II. Title
TX823.W48 1995
641.5'78--dc20   95-38933
                                                        CIP
                                                        AC

To my mother, who introduced me to campfire cooking,
and my family, who carries on the tradition.
L. W.

To my mother, Evelyn Lee, whose artistry always tastes delicious.
F. L.

CONTENTS

"Hi! My name is Rikki. Ready to cook on a stick?"

COOKING OVER A CAMPFIRE

Campers do it.
Cowpokes do it.
City people sometimes travel miles to do it.

They all cook over a campfire. Sometimes they roast marshmallows in the middle of a forest. Other times they grill salmon in a city park. Whatever they are preparing, it always tastes better cooked out-of-doors. Fresh air and the smell of wood smoke stir the appetite. Without refrigerators, stoves, or microwaves, outdoor cooks can create great meals—sometimes even better than the ones at home!

With this book, you can do it, too. Your cookout might be at a campground with other campers, in the forest with your scouting group, or in your own backyard with your family. Wherever it is, cooking outdoors should be as hassle-free as possible. The recipes in this book are meant to be simple to prepare. The ingredients require little cutting, and the cooking requires little cleanup.

You'll learn to make some cooking equipment and build a campfire. Next, you'll learn some ways to cook, using a stick, a pouch, and a grill. Then just follow the recipes. Soon you'll be as comfortable eating outdoors as the animals who live there.

Mealtime is more fun if you prepare for your cookout ahead of time. Make and collect the equipment you need, gather sticks, and cut and mix the ingredients for the recipes you have chosen before you head outside. (It's a good idea for all chefs, whether cooking indoors or out, to read through the entire recipe before beginning to cook. That way you'll know what things must be done ahead of time, what equipment you need to gather, and if you have enough time to do the cooking.)

Having a parent or other adult helper with you is a must. Not only is it more fun to be together, but there are things you will want help with—like knowing where it is safe to build a campfire, cutting and measuring ingredients, putting out the fire, and, especially, cleaning up. When you see this symbol ⬛══▬ within a recipe, that means cutting food with a sharp knife is required. Make sure to ask for adult help with cutting, and always use caution when handling a knife. Getting hungry? Let's get started!

CAMPFIRES

You can build campfires in most picnic areas and campgrounds. If you see a sign like this, 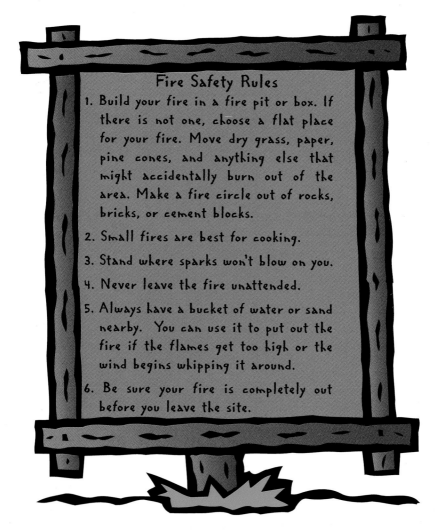 look for another place.

Every outdoor cook needs to know the rules:

Fire Safety Rules

1. Build your fire in a fire pit or box. If there is not one, choose a flat place for your fire. Move dry grass, paper, pine cones, and anything else that might accidentally burn out of the area. Make a fire circle out of rocks, bricks, or cement blocks.

2. Small fires are best for cooking.

3. Stand where sparks won't blow on you.

4. Never leave the fire unattended.

5. Always have a bucket of water or sand nearby. You can use it to put out the fire if the flames get too high or the wind begins whipping it around.

6. Be sure your fire is completely out before you leave the site.

Gathering Firewood

To make a good campfire, you first need to gather three kinds of fuel:

tinder

"Anything that burns is called fuel."

kindling

logs

Tinder is the first fuel you put in the fire box or fire circle. It should be something small that burns quickly. Twigs, dry grass, pine cones, even crumpled sheets of newspaper are good tinder.

On top of that put slightly larger pieces of wood that will burn longer. These "kindle" the flame, keeping it going until the larger wood catches fire. Bigger twigs and sticks will work.

Next is the wood that will cook your food, usually small logs. Hardwoods such as oak and maple are best for cooking fires. The coals of these woods burn slowly, giving you more cooking time. In many areas, cottonwood and pine are the available woods. Those softwoods burn quickly. If you use them, have all your food ready so you can begin cooking as soon as the coals reach the right stage.

Some places have no wood at all. On the treeless plains, Indians and pioneers had to cook over a fire made of "buffalo chips" (dried manure). You could use charcoal instead.

Building the Fire

There are many kinds of campfires. Some are built in a hole and some are shaped like an "A" and blaze high to keep you warm. But the "log cabin" fire is one of the best fires to cook over. It is slow burning and, as the fuel burns down, provides a thick bed of hot coals.

1. Make a small pile of tinder, then stack kindling around the outside, leaning the wood toward the center in the shape of a tepee.

2. Pile logs around the tepee as if you were building a tiny log cabin.

3. As the cabin gets taller, gradually place the logs a little closer to the tepee.

4. Add logs until the cabin is about as tall as your knees.

5. Strike a safety match, which is coated so that it will light only on the striking plate on the match box, and carefully light the tinder.

(1)   (2-4)

If firewood isn't available, use charcoal piled in a pyramid. Follow the directions on the charcoal bag. Some charcoal requires the use of lighter fluid, while other kinds come ready to light. **Ask an adult to apply the lighter fluid. Do not add any fluid after you have struck a match.**

Campers, cowpokes, city slickers, and kids all have to be patient. It takes a while for the campfire to get to the cooking stage. The time varies with the kind of wood you use, but it is usually 20 to 30 minutes. Even if those you are cooking for are holding their plates, drooling, and asking, "Isn't that fire ready yet?" don't start cooking until the flames die down and just coals are left, or you will burn your food. Set the table and get the ingredients ready while you wait. When the flames die down and the coals glow red with white edges, it's time to cook your grub.

"Don't light the fire until a grown-up says it's okay. If you haven't used a match before, an adult can show you how."

Putting Out the Fire

After your meal and before you leave your cooking site, you must put out the campfire.

1. Use a stick to spread the coals into a thin layer.

2. Sprinkle water or dirt over all of the coals. Don't pour a large amount of water on the coals all at once. It makes steam that could burn you or others standing nearby.

3. Stir the coals and add more water or dirt until the coals are cool enough to touch. An adult can help you with this.

4. Be sure to carry out all trash or put it in trash bins. Leave the site clean for the next campfire cook.

Cooking Time

Many of the recipes that follow give an approximate cooking time. The actual time is affected by many things, including how hot the coals are, how far above them you hold your food, even how high up in the mountains or close to the sea you are. The cooking times given are for wood fires. If you are using charcoal, the time will be about half the given time. An adult, even if he or she is a city slicker, can help you decide when the food is ready to eat.

COOKING EQUIPMENT

Before going on a cookout, there are some things you need to make and gather.

Cooking sticks will be used to cook many recipes in this book. The right kind of sticks are not always available at campsites, so make your own reusable "forest cooking stick." Instructions are on page 15.

 Oven mitts and **barbecue cooking tools** help protect your hands from the heat of the campfire. Oven mitts are thick, padded mittens. Use them when handling hot foods and cooking tools. Be careful to keep them away from the flames. (Remember, if sparks or flames land on your mitts or clothing, use your bucket of water to drench the item immediately.) Barbecue tool sets have long-handled turners, tongs, and forks. Using them allows you to stand back from the fire to tend your food.

 **Aluminum foil** is a valuable tool around the camp. You can cook meals in it, make cooking and serving containers, and wrap leftovers to take home. Heavy-duty foil works best, but three layers of regular-strength foil can also be used.

 Most campsites have **metal grates** to cook on, but not all. Metal grates are hard to find in the forest or out on the range, so consider taking your own. A variety of inexpensive **wire cooking grills** are available at outdoor shops. If you buy a medium- or large-sized grill, you'll be able to cook more food at once. You can also use it to hold your food over the fire when your arm gets tired or you need to do something else.

 You probably have **measuring cups and spoons** at home. If not, purchase a set of each. Measuring-cup sets usually contain cups to measure 1/8, 1/4, 1/2, and 1 cup. They fit neatly inside each other, so they don't take up much room. Spoon sets contain 1/4, 1/2, 1 teaspoon, and 1 tablespoon measures. When you measure, fill the cup or spoon to the top and level the ingredients with a stick or the back of a table knife.

Sealable plastic bags in pint, quart, 1/2-gallon, and gallon sizes have many uses while camping. You can mix and season ingredients in them. You can also use them for storing leftovers and separating wet or dirty items, such as dirty silverware, wet bathing suits, or messy cleanup rags. Use the ones marked "freezer bags." They are heavier than the regular ones and shouldn't split while you are mixing or carrying foods.

 **A first-aid kit** should be on hand to treat cuts, burns, and insect bites. A kit might include bandages, antiseptic ointment, aspirin, and calamine lotion. Purchase a first-aid kit from a drugstore or outdoor shop, or make your own. Find out how from a book about first aid, available at your library or bookstore.

If you are traveling to your cookout, many of the foods that you will be taking need to be kept cold until they are used. (The labels on most foods will tell you if they need to be refrigerated.) **An insulated plastic storage chest** with some ice packs will usually do the trick.

PACKING LIST

For cooking:

safety matches
aluminum foil
oven mitt
can opener
knife
paper towels
long-handled turner and tongs
measuring cups and spoons
wire grill
bucket or pitcher for water
bucket of sand
spatula
cooking sticks and holders
coat hangers
newspaper
nonstick cooking spray

For eating:

plates
napkins
silverware
glasses
table cover
salt, pepper, other seasonings
drinks
dressings: mayonnaise, catsup,
   mustard, barbecue sauce, etc.

For cleanup:

sealable plastic bags
   (for leftovers)
plastic garbage bags
   (large ones for trash; smaller
   ones for dirty dishes and to
   carry recyclable items)
biodegradable soap
dishcloth
washtub

Miscellaneous:

first-aid kit
extra hangers
firewood or charcoal
shovel
flashlight, lantern with extra
   batteries
camera and film
sunscreen and insect repellent
insulated plastic storage chest
ice packs

COOKING ON A STICK

Sticks were probably the first cooking tools. In prehistoric times, cave dwellers may have roasted woolly mammoth steaks on sticks. People have cooked on them ever since.

The kind of cooking stick you need depends on what you will cook. A long, thin stick with a sharpened end is good for cooking a single hot dog or marshmallow. Several hot dogs or marshmallows, or a larger piece of meat like a pork chop, can be stuck onto a forked stick. A variety of meats and vegetables can be put on a thin stick to make a kabob.

A cooking stick should be green (growing) wood. Green wood doesn't burn easily. Willow grows along many stream banks. It is a good choice, but any green, nonpoisonous wood will work. Cut your stick about 3 feet long. It should be thick enough that it won't bend when you put your food on it. Ask an adult to help you whittle one end to a point using a sharp knife.

If you make some reusable forest cooking sticks from clean coat hangers, you won't have to look for sticks each time.

Forest Cooking Stick

You'll need to ask an adult for help with this project.

1. Cut the bottom of a wire coat hanger in two.

2. Straighten the cut sides.

3. Twist the two sides together. A stick inserted through the hook may help you twist.

4. Stop twisting about four inches from the end.

5. Bend the two ends into a fork shape.

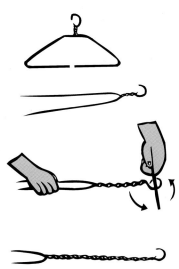

- **Beware!** The handle of your stick will get hot as you cook with it. Always use your oven mitt to hold it.

- Wash your cooking stick with hot, soapy water after each use. If the coating on your stick ever begins to peel, sand it smooth with sandpaper.

- When cooking on a stick, gradually turn the stick in your hands so all sides of the food get cooked.

- If you don't want to hold the stick, prop it between two large rocks so that the food hangs over the fire ring or box. If you are using a twig or branch as your cooking stick, you can place your food in the middle of your stick and perch the stick on two forked sticks stuck in the ground on either side of the fire.

Now you're ready to cook. Since there are no more woolly mammoths, let's start with something else.

Beary Basic Biscuit Mix

Beary Basic Biscuit Mix will be used to make many of the recipes in this book. Make it at home and use it as you need it. Store it in a cool, dry place and it will be good for a few weeks.

What you need:

6 cups flour
1 cup nonfat dry milk
1/4 cup baking powder
1 teaspoon salt
1 cup shortening

What you do:

1. Put all ingredients into a 1-gallon, sealable plastic bag.

2. Press air out of bag and seal. Squeeze ingredients together until well mixed.

3. When ready to use, mix 1/3 cup water with 2 cups mix to make biscuit dough. Or you can make pancake batter by adding 1 egg and 1 1/2 cups of water to 2 cups of mix.

"When mixing, always hold the plastic bag upright and squeeze gently. That way, if the bag comes unsealed, its contents won't spill into your hiking boots."

Snail on a Limb

(Stick) Serves 4

What you need:

2 cups Beary Basic Biscuit Mix
1/3 cup water
Nonstick cooking spray

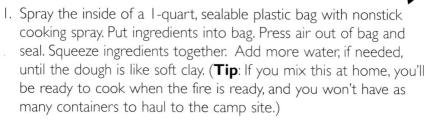

What you do:

1. Spray the inside of a 1-quart, sealable plastic bag with nonstick cooking spray. Put ingredients into bag. Press air out of bag and seal. Squeeze ingredients together. Add more water, if needed, until the dough is like soft clay. (**Tip**: If you mix this at home, you'll be ready to cook when the fire is ready, and you won't have as many containers to haul to the camp site.)

2. Roll a handful of the mixture into a snake shape about 8 inches long.

3. Coil the dough in a tight, snail-like spiral around your cooking stick.

4. Hold dough low over hot coals (but not touching them). Turn the stick as the dough cooks. The dough will start to get crusty, then turn darker. It's ready when it is golden brown all over (about 8 minutes).

Pull the snail off the limb to eat. **Careful, it's hot!**

Try these:

Bite one end off the cooked snail, and if the hole in the middle is big enough, stuff it with butter and jelly or ham and cheese.

Want a Caterpillar in a Cocoon? Push a hot dog or precooked sausage onto the end of your cooking stick. Cook it over coals, turning to cook evenly, until bubbles form on the skin. Wrap dough in a spiral around the hot dog or sausage just as you did for the Snail on a Limb and cook until the dough is crusty and golden brown.

If you want a regular hot dog, just put the cooked hot dog in a bun and add mustard, catsup, pickles, and onions—or whatever you like!

"Try putting a slice of cheese around the hot dog before you wrap the dough."

"A poke is a bag or sack."

Porky in a Poke

(Stick) Serves 4   *Main Dish*

What you need:

2 cups Beary Basic Biscuit Mix
2/3 cup water
4 hot dogs
I small can refried beans
4 slices American cheese
Nonstick cooking spray

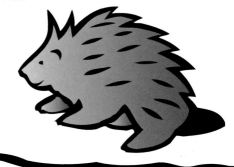

What you do:

1. Spray the inside of a 1-quart, sealable plastic bag with nonstick cooking spray. Put the biscuit mix and water in bag. Press air out of bag and seal. Squeeze bag until ingredients are well mixed.

2. Pinch dough into 4 small pieces and flatten into rectangles.

3. On each piece of dough put I strip of cheese and I tablespoon refried beans.

4. Push a hot dog onto your stick and cook it over the coals, turning it to cook evenly.

5. Lay the hot dog (still on the stick) on top of dough, cheese, and beans.

6. Dip your finger in a little bit of water and run it around the dough rectangle to make it sticky. Then press edges together to seal the hot dog, beans, and cheese inside the dough.

7. Cook over coals until dough is crusty and golden brown.

Moose Kabobs

(Stick) Serves 4   Main dish

What you need:

1 pound beefsteak
4 cups cut vegetables
  (choose from onions, bell peppers, zucchini,
  mushrooms, and cherry tomatoes)
1 cup French, Russian, or Italian salad dressing

What you do:

The day before:

1. Cut steak and vegetables into 1-inch chunks. Ask an adult to help
   you with this. If you have permission to use a sharp knife, place
   meat or vegetables on a cutting board to cut. Keep your fingers
   away from the knife blade.

2. Put meat and vegetables into a 1-quart, sealable plastic bag.
   Add dressing.

3. Seal the bag and keep in refrigerator or ice chest until time to
   use.

At camp:

1. Skewer (push) meat and vegetables onto smooth sticks. Use thin,
   green twigs or branches you've collected, or buy wooden kabob
   skewers at the grocery store.

2. Cook over hot coals. Turn every 3–4 minutes and cook until all
   sides are done (about 10 minutes).

Try this:

*Shrimp or hot dogs can be used instead of beefsteak. Some people like ham
and pineapple kabobs.*

S'mores

(Stick) Serves 1   *Dessert*

This recipe has been cooked over most every campfire ever made. Make it, and you'll know why.

What you need:

1 whole graham cracker (about 2 1/2 by 5 inches)

1/2 flat milk chocolate candy bar, with or without nuts (the whole
   chocolate bar should be about the same size
   as the graham cracker)

1 marshmallow

"Take extra supplies. You're sure to want s'more."

What you do:

1. Break the graham cracker in half.

2. Place the half chocolate bar on one piece of cracker. Set aside.

3. Put marshmallow on a stick. Toast it over coals until golden brown.

4. Put marshmallow on top of chocolate and cracker and top with other graham cracker half.

5. Press together and hold for about 30 seconds while the marshmallow melts the chocolate. Eat!

    Careful—the marshmallow stays hot for a long time.

⭐ Ranger's Apple Pie ⭐

(Stick) Serves 1　　　　　　　　　　　　　　　　　*Dessert*

An apple pie turned inside out!

What you need:

1 cooking apple (Granny Smith,
  Jonathan, or Rome apple)
1/8 cup sugar
1 tablespoon brown sugar
1 teaspoon cinnamon

What you do:

1. Combine sugar, brown sugar, and cinnamon in a 1-pint, sealable plastic bag and set aside.

2. Place apple on cooking stick.

3. Roast 4 inches over coals, gradually turning apple so all sides will cook. Roast until the skin puckers all over, about 15 minutes.

4. Carefully pull off the skin, using a fork or small stick. If the peel doesn't come off easily, cook the apple a little longer. You may want an adult to help remove the skin.

5. Put apple into open plastic bag (leave it on the stick!) and roll in sugar mixture until coated.

6. Return apple to heat, turning slowly, allowing sugar to melt (about 2 minutes).

7. Eat it in a bowl or off your stick after it has cooled.

COOKING IN A POUCH

Some foods taste best when cooked covered. Long ago, people wrapped their food in leaves or clay. Today, we can cook in an aluminum-foil pouch. Cooking and cleanup are easy, and the foil is recyclable.

Here's how to make a foil pouch:

1. Tear off a piece of heavy-duty aluminum foil two times as big as what you are going to wrap.
2. Put the foil down, shiny side up.
3. Place food in center of foil.
4. Bring two opposite sides of foil together. Fold or roll foil down to the food.
5. Gently flatten the ends of the pouch.
6. Roll the ends toward the center. The bundle should now be tightly sealed.

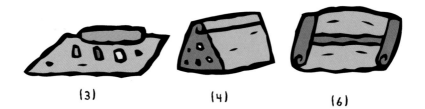

(3)   (4)   (6)

The pouch with the food can be hung from a stick and held over the fire. However, it is easier to place it right in the coals to cook. With your cooking tools, cover the bundle with the hot coals so that it cooks evenly. Use long-handled tongs or a turner (even a shovel) to move the pouch (but don't puncture the foil!). Be careful not to touch the fire.

"Charcoal briquettes burn very hot, much hotter than wood. If you are cooking over charcoal, wrap your pouch again in 3 sheets of newspaper, then in another foil pouch. That should keep your food from burning."

Forget to bring a bowl? You can make one! Cut a 12-inch square piece of heavy foil and mold it around a round rock, a log, or even your bent knee. Fold the foil edges down and flatten the bottom. Your bowl is ready to be filled with chili, vegetables, or almost anything. After you've eaten, rinse the bowl, crumple it, and put it in your recycle bag.

Make a cup the same way Shape a 12-inch square piece of foil over the end of a small round log. Roll the top edges down, flatten the bottom and you've got a cup.

Then try this recipe: rest the cup in hot coals or on the grill, fill it with milk, and heat it until it just begins to steam. Carefully use your tongs to remove the cup of milk from the heat. Don't squeeze the cup so tight that it collapses. Stir in half a chocolate bar, and sip the best hot chocolate you ever had.

Wh-o-o's Chili?

(Pouch) Serves 4 to 6   *Main dish*

This is a great recipe to make on a starry night when there's a chill in the air. While the chili cooks, wrap up in a blanket and watch the sky. You might see falling stars or, if you are very lucky, an owl gliding silently through the night.

What you need:

1 pound ground beef
1 16-ounce can beans in chili sauce
1 8-ounce can tomato sauce
1/2 onion, cut up (if you like)

What you do:

1. Put all ingredients in a 1-gallon, sealable plastic bag.
2. Seal the bag and gently squeeze ingredients together.
3. Pour mixture onto 18 x 18-inch piece of foil and seal.
4. Cook in coals for about 30 minutes.

Angler's Favorite Beans

(Pouch) Serves 4   *Vegetable*

These steaming beans are perfect to serve with the catch of the day. You can also pile them next to any of the hot dog or hamburger dishes for a great outdoor meal.

What you need:

1 16-ounce can baked beans
1/2 medium onion, chopped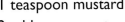
1 teaspoon mustard
2 tablespoons catsup
1 tablespoon brown sugar

What you do:

1. Put beans and other ingredients in a 1-quart, sealable plastic bag. Squeeze bag gently until ingredients are mixed.

2. Pour ingredients onto a 12-inch square piece of foil, fold into a pouch, and seal.

3. Cook in coals until heated through (about 15 minutes).

Try this:

Make this a main dish by adding four hot dogs cut in 1-inch slices before you seal the pouch.

Cozy Caves

(Pouch) Serves 3   *Main dish*

What you need:

1 pound ground beef
1 egg
Dash of salt and pepper
3 large onions, peeled

What you do:

At home:

1. Put ground beef, egg, salt, and pepper into a 1-quart, sealable plastic bag, seal, and squeeze together until mixed. Set aside.

2. With a knife, cut the onions in half, between the ends.

3. Remove the onion insides, leaving a shell about 1/2 inch thick.

4. Mound three onion halves with meat mixture and top with another onion shell.

5. Wrap each onion in a foil pouch. Keep cold in refrigerator or ice chest.

At camp:

1. Place each pouch in coals and cook for 15 minutes.

2. Turn upside down and cook for 15 minutes more. Use long-handled tongs to move pouches. They're hot!

Veggie Herd

(Pouch) Serves 4   *Vegetable*

What you need:

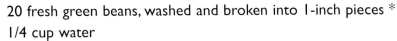

4 medium potatoes, washed *
20 fresh green beans, washed and broken into 1-inch pieces *
1/4 cup water
1/4 cup crumbled or grated cheddar or monterey jack cheese
1 teaspoon herb seasoning
Salt

What you do:

1. Cut each potato into eight pieces.
2. Place pieces on top of piece of foil, about 12 × 18 inches.
3. Add green beans to potatoes.
4. Sprinkle with salt, seasoning, water, and cheese.
5. Seal foil pouch.
6. Cook covered in coals about 30 minutes.

"Try it with barbecue sauce."

* Canned sliced potatoes and green beans can be used. Canned vegetables don't need to cook as long as fresh ones—about 20 minutes instead of 30.

Chameleon Dinner

(Pouch) Serves 1   *Main dish*

This is a basic recipe that can change every time you make it. Just use different meat and vegetables. Try chicken and carrots one time, pork and asparagus the next.

What you need:

1/4 pound boneless meat (choose one): chicken strips, hamburger
   patty, cubed pork, fish
1/3 cup chopped fresh or canned vegetables (choose one):
   green beans, peas, carrots, asparagus, mixed vegetables
Slices of onion (if you like)
2 tablespoons dry gravy mix or onion soup mix
Salt and pepper to taste
1/3 cup sliced fresh or canned potatoes
2 tablespoons water (3 tablespoons if you use
   fresh vegetables)

What you do:

1. Put all ingredients on an 18-inch-square piece of foil.

2. Fold and seal foil.

3. Set in coals, cover with more hot coals (use your tongs!), and
   cook about 20–30 minutes.

4. Using long-handled tongs, remove from fire, slit pouch, and dig in.

"You could prepare this recipe at home and seal it in a 1/2-gallon plastic bag. At the campsite, just empty it onto the foil, fold into a pouch, and cook."

Forget your eating utensils? Try making a pair of woodsy eating sticks. Cut two smooth sticks about the size of a pencil. Holding both sticks in one hand, practice using them like chopsticks. Try to grip firmer foods like meat between the sticks. Use the sticks as a scoop for softer foods, such as cooked potatoes.

☆Honey Bear's Delight☆

(Pouch) Serves 1   *Fruit*

What you need:

1 apple, cut in small pieces
1/4 cup raisins
1/8 cup chopped nuts
3 marshmallows
1 teaspoon butter
1 tablespoon honey or syrup

"Careful, it's hot!"

What you do:

1. Put apples, raisins, nuts, marshmallows, and butter on a piece of foil 12 inches square.

2. Drizzle honey or syrup on top.

3. Fold foil into a pouch and place it in hot coals.

4. Cook 10 minutes, remove, open, and enjoy.

At dawn and again at dusk, animals make their way to water for a cooling drink. You might see them or their tracks along the bank of a stream or lake. Can you identify the tracks? If you see tracks like this, there's a bear nearby. Don't follow those tracks!

Hibernating Bananas

(Pouch) Serves 1 · *Fruit dessert*

These are almost as popular as s'mores.

What you need:

1 banana
1/2 flat, milk chocolate candy bar, broken into pieces
1/8 cup miniature marshmallows

What you do:

1. Peel back one section of banana peel, but don't remove it.

2. Slice across banana, making 1-inch pieces. Remove every other chunk. You can eat those now.

3. Fill the holes between the remaining banana pieces with chocolate and marshmallows.

4. Replace peel and wrap in foil.

5. Place wrapped banana in coals.

6. Let bananas hibernate about 10 minutes, until chocolate and marshmallows are melted.

Hop Toad Popcorn

(Pouch) Serves 3

What you need:
1/3 cup vegetable oil
1/2 cup popping corn
1/2 teaspoon salt
2 tablespoons parmesan cheese

What you do:

1. Put oil, corn, and salt in center of 18–inch square piece of foil.

2. Fold into pouch, carefully turning down all seams just twice so steam won't escape. The pouch will seem too big for the corn, but the corn needs room to pop!

3. Push pouch onto cooking stick by poking stick through the center of the top, just under the fold.

4. Hold low over hot coals, shaking gently and constantly. Soon you will hear popping.

5. When popping stops or slows to more than 5 seconds between pops, open pouch carefully and add parmesan cheese.

Squirrel Nibbles

(Pouch) Serves 1   *Vegetable*

What you need:

1 ear of corn
1 teaspoon butter
Salt

What you do:

1. Shuck an ear of corn by pulling the husks and strings off.

2. Top with butter and sprinkle with salt.

3. Wrap corn in foil.

4. Cook covered in coals for about 15 minutes. Be careful when you unwrap and eat it—it will be hot!

Try this:

Corn on the cob is great just with a little butter, but if you want something different, try adding some chopped green onions, crushed garlic, or fresh herbs such as sage, thyme, or basil to the pouch before sealing it.

People aren't the only ones attracted to the smell of campfire food. At a family picnic, a deer may stand beside your table staring at your food, while a squirrel chatters from the other side of the table, and a camp robber (a kind of jaybird) clings shrieking to a branch above. They are all waiting to see what tidbits might be left behind.

It's tempting to feed wild animals, but it's better for them if you don't. Animals that are fed people-food forget how to find wild-animal food. They can become campground pests or, worse, might starve during the long winter when people aren't around to feed them. Besides, wild animals have sharp teeth, and they bite

COOKING ON A GRATE OR GRILL

Grilling is one of the most popular ways to cook outdoors. You can cook practically anything on a grill, from pizza to grilled peanut-butter-and-bologna sandwiches—if that's what you like. You can even use pots and pans on a grill. But the recipes in this section will show you how to cook the food right on the grill (that way, you don't have to wash those messy pots and pans!).

Prepare the wood or charcoal fire as before. When the coals are ready, glowing red with white edges, position the metal grate 4 to 6 inches above them. If the campsite doesn't have a grate, rest your own wire grill on the fire ring, fire box, or the rocks that make up your fire ring. Ask your adult to help you make sure the grill doesn't wobble. You don't want your meal tipping into the fire. Cook your food directly on the grill. Food in foil pouches can be cooked this way, too—just cook it longer than you would in the hot coals.

Probably the simplest food to cook over the grill is a hamburger. You might try that first.

Bucky Burgers

(Grill) Serves 1   *Main dish*

Sink your teeth into this gourmet hamburger.

What you need:

1/4 pound ground beef

1/4 cup filling (choose and chop two or
  three of the following to make 1/4 cup):
    onion, olives, sunflower seeds, celery, car-
    rots, mushrooms

What you do:

1. Make a ball of the hamburger.

2. With your thumbs, hollow out a well in the center of the meatball.

3. Put filling into the well.

4. Press the sides of the meat around the filling to close.

5. Flatten meat into patty.

6. Cook on grill for about 5 minutes.

7. Using a long-handled turner, turn the patty and cook about 5 more minutes.

Tip: *Since cooking time varies, watch your burger carefully. Make sure it is cooked all the way through, until there is no pink meat left in the center.*

Try these:

Serve with Squirrel Nibbles (page 35) and Honey Bear's Delight (page 32) or other side dishes, or on a bun dressed as you like it.

Need something to munch on before your burger? Make some nachos by spreading a layer of tortilla chips on foil on a grill. Sprinkle with cheese and cook until cheese melts. ***Careful!*** *The foil will be very hot.*

Bird's Nest Breakfast

(Grill) Serves 2   *Breakfast*

What you need:

1 large navel orange (thick-skinned)
1/2 cup canned shoestring potatoes (the crunchy kind)
1/2 cup chopped ham or sliced ham lunch meat
2 eggs
Salt and pepper
1 tablespoon milk or water

What you do:

1. Cut the orange in half.

2. Using a spoon or your fingers, scoop out the inside of the orange. Put the orange insides into a bowl and set aside to have with breakfast.

3. Combine eggs, a dash of salt and pepper, and a tablespoon of milk or water in a 1-quart, sealable plastic bag. Zip the bag shut.

4. Gently squeeze and shake egg mixture until yolks are broken and everything is mixed.

5. Pour half of the mixture into each orange shell.

6. Using long-handled tongs, gently set shells on grill.

7. Cook until eggs are firm, about 10 minutes, and remove the shells from the grill with the tongs.

8. To serve, mound shoestring potatoes onto plate. Top with ham (if you want it warm, put it in a pouch and set it in the coals while your egg is cooking). Then scoop egg out of shell onto potatoes and ham. Breakfast is ready. Start pecking!

Loony Eggs

There are many ways to cook eggs over a campfire. One Middle Eastern recipe calls for two eggs to be stuffed into a fish. The fish is put into a chicken, the chicken into a sheep, and the whole sheep into a camel. The camel is then roasted over a fire for four or five days! Loony Eggs are simpler and a lot faster.

What you need:

1 egg
1 piece of bread
Butter
Nonstick cooking spray

"Try using a cookie cutter to make the hole in the bread. Your Loony Egg can look like a dinosaur, a star, or even a howling dog!"

What you do:

1. Spray a 6 x 12-inch piece of foil with cooking spray. **Never spray nonstick cooking spray near the fire.**

2. Put foil on the grill, sprayed side up.

3. Butter both sides of the bread.

4. Tear a hole in the middle of the bread (about 2 inches across). Eat the "hole." (No, you're not finished!)

5. Put bread on right side of foil.

6. Crack an egg into the bread hole. Cook until clear egg "white" turns white.

7. Put turner under foil, bread, and egg and carefully fold onto left side of foil.

8. Cook about 1 minute for you runny-yolk folks, 2 minutes if you like your egg firm, 3 if you like the eggs to bounce off the plate.

Bandit's Stuffed Fish

(Grill) Serves 2 to 3   *Main dish*

Raccoons aren't the only ones that like fresh fish. There's nothing better than grilling a fish you just caught from a high mountain lake or a swift-moving stream. After you've cleaned the fish, try this tasty recipe. If you prefer to leave the angling to others, you can grill a small, whole, store-bought fish, such as trout, salmon, or catfish.

What you need:
Cleaned fish, about 1 1/4 pounds
Juice from 1/2 lemon
1/2 cup chopped celery
1/2 cup chopped onion
1/4 cup chopped mushrooms
1/4 cup slivered almonds
Salt and pepper and herb seasoning to taste
1/4 cup olive or vegetable oil
2 toothpicks

What you do:

Ahead of time:

1. Seal fish, oil, and lemon juice in a 1-quart, sealable plastic bag. This can be done an hour or a day ahead of time. Keep fish in ice chest until ready to cook.

2. Carefully chop the celery, onion, and mushrooms. When using a sharp knife, always cut away from your body. Ask an adult to help you with all this chopping. Seal ingredients in a 1-quart, sealable plastic bag. Take fish bag and stuffing bag to campsite.

At camp:

1. Sprinkle the inside of fish with salt and pepper.

2. Stuff the inside with chopped celery, onion, mushrooms, and slivered almonds. Use toothpicks to hold the cavity closed.

3. Grill fish for 5 to 8 minutes. Carefully turn fish over, keeping the fish spine to the grill so the stuffing won't fall out. Cook until done (the fish should flake when stuck with a fork).

Foxy Pizza

(Grill) Serves 2 to 3   *Main dish*

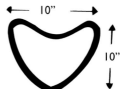

What you need:

1 cup Beary Basic Biscuit Mix

1/3 cup water

1 cup pizza sauce

6 ounces cooked meat (a variety of cooked meats are available at your grocery store; try precooked sausage, sliced pepperoni, or canned chicken)

4 ounces grated mozzarella cheese

Small amounts of other things you like on pizza—maybe chopped olives, onions, and bell peppers

Nonstick cooking spray

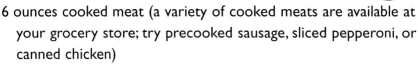

What you do:

Ahead of time:

1. Spray the inside of a 1-quart plastic bag with nonstick cooking spray. Put Beary Basic Biscuit Mix and water into bag and squeeze ingredients together. Set aside.

2. Carefully chop the ingredients you want on your pizza and seal them in a plastic bag. Set aside.

3. Using plain paper, draw and cut out fox head pattern, following the shape and size indicated in the drawing above.

At the cook-out:

1. Tear off a large sheet of foil, about 12 x 12 inches.

2. Spray foil with nonstick cooking spray (but not near the fire).

3. Dump dough onto foil. Use a spoon to remove any dough that sticks to the bag.

4. Flatten dough, patting and stretching it into a rounded triangle (about 10 inches across the top, 10 inches from top to bottom, and 1/8 inch thick).

5. Lay fox pattern on top of dough. Using a table knife, cut out the shape of a fox head. Remove dough that is not the fox. You can make another small pizza out of that, but cook it in its own foil.

6. When coals are ready, carefully put foil with fox-shaped dough on the grate.

7. Tear off another sheet of foil (12 x 12 inches), spray with nonstick cooking spray, and put it on top of foxy dough. Cook the dough about 5 minutes.

8. Slide a long-handled turner under the bottom piece of foil and flip over, being careful that the dough doesn't slide out. This is tricky. You might want help.

9. Remove top foil, fold in half, and set aside.

10. Cover fox crust with pizza sauce, meat, chosen vegetables, and cheese, in that order. **Be careful when you add each ingredient—the grill is hot!** Set aside a little meat and other ingredients to finish the fox face.

11. Open extra piece of foil and place it over the pizza like a tent.

12. Cook 10 to 12 minutes, or until cheese melts thoroughly.

13. Remove from grill and decorate fox's face.

Try this:

For a quick, round pizza, use a large tortilla in place of the biscuit mix.

"Make this pizza any shape that doesn't have small, protruding parts. How about a bear face, a crescent moon, or dad's funny fishing hat?"

TASTY SNACKS AND TRAIL FOOD

Whatever you like to do outdoors—hike, fish, watch wildlife, even doze in a hammock—you are bound to get hungry. Make these no-cook recipes to snack on at camp or on the trail You could also use them to complete your meal.

Moose Lips

The outdoors is a place you can be a little silly and try new things. Moose lips are a pretty silly new thing.

What you need:
I apple with red skin (do not peel)
Peanut butter
Mini-marshmallows

What you do:

1. Carefully cut apple into eight pieces. Be sure to get help if you need it.

2. Remove the core from each piece by cutting out the center area that holds the seeds.

3. Smear one side of each slice with peanut butter.

4. Push a row of mini-marshmallows into the peanut butter of 4 apple slices.

5. Top each slice with another apple slice, peanut-butter side down, matching top and bottom shapes. You should have something that resembles a moose mouth staring back at you. Eat!

GORP

Good Old Raisins and Peanuts

(No Cook) Serves many   *Snack*

Your feet ache. Sweat trickles down your neck. Mosquitoes buzz in your ears. The trail is lost in a jumble of bushes and trees. Your father says, "Never fear, I'll get us back!" Aren't you glad you brought along a bag of GORP?

What you need:

2 cups roasted peanuts

1/2 cup raisins

1 cup of any of the following that you like:

> Chocolate candies
>
> Licorice bites
>
> Chocolate chips
>
> Other nuts (pecans, cashews)
>
> Seeds (dried sunflower or pumpkin seeds)
>
> Dried fruit (banana chips, apricots, apples)
>
> Pretzels, sesame sticks, dry cereal

What you do:

1. Pour ingredients into 1/2-gallon, sealable plastic bag and mix.

2. Pack in small pocket-sized bags to take along on hikes or anywhere you'll get hungry.

"Take a Hike" Salad

(No Cook) Serves 1   *Snack/side dish*

What you need:

Large apple
Filling 1: peanut butter and raisins
Filling 2: cottage cheese, raisins, and nuts

What you do:

1. Cut the top off a large apple and ask an adult to core it.

2. Fill center with peanut butter and raisins

   or

   2 tablespoons of cottage cheese, one tablespoon raisins, and one tablespoon of nuts   or

   invent your own filling. You might try chocolate chips, honey, yogurt, marshmallows, sunflower seeds, chopped celery, tuna fish, or cheese.
   Anyone want to try potato chips?

3. Hold this in your hand and eat it on the go.

"Remember, if you use cottage cheese, yogurt, mayonnaise, or any dairy product, keep your 'take a hike' salad in the ice chest until you are ready to eat it."

Deer Baubles

(No Cook) Serves 1   *Snack*

What you need:
1/2 cup dry cereal that has holes
1/4 cup mixed dried fruit (apricots, apples, pineapple)

What you do:
1. Tie one piece of cereal onto one end of a 28-inch piece of cotton string or dental floss. Careful, don't break the cereal! Leave at least a 1-inch tail.

2. Thread the string through a large needle.

3. Thread the cereal and fruit onto the string in any design, making a long chain.

4. When you have just an inch or two of string left, pull the needle off the thread and tie the ends of the string together.

5. Wear the edible "baubles" around your neck, nibbling from the string when you're hungry for a snack. Or have the baubles with a glass of milk for breakfast.

"Don't add berries you find growing in the forest unless an adult can tell you that they are safe to eat. Many wild berries are poisonous. You could get 'berry' sick."